Asleep

IN THE
LAND *of* NOD

THIRTY DAYS OF PRAYER TOWARD
AWAKENING THE CHURCH

DAVID BUTTS

PRAYERSHOP
PUBLISHING

TERRE HAUTE, INDIANA

Multiple Quantity Discounts are available for this product at prayershop.org.

PrayerShop Publishing is the publishing arm of the Church Prayer Leaders Network. The Church Prayer Leaders Network exists to equip and inspire local churches and their prayer leaders in their desire to disciple their people in prayer and to become a "house of prayer for all nations." Its online store, prayershop.org, has more than 150 prayer resources available for purchase or download.

ISBN: 978-1-935012-71-9

HOW TO USE THIS GUIDE

The word has gotten out in the Church. We need revival! No longer is it just a nice idea. There's a renewed sense of desperation. Christians are beginning to pray about issues relating to revival.

That's what this devotional is about—ways to help you pray passionately about another Great Awakening in the Church and the nation.

Before beginning this devotional, please read the introduction that speaks of the great need for revival today. May these introductory words build in your life an even greater desire to see the Church awakened from its slumber!

Next, set aside a time each day to pull this guide out and focus on one day's content. Read the content prayerfully, asking the Holy Spirit to speak to your heart. Then let the prayer focus and prayer stimulate a time of prayer for revival in the Church. Throughout the 30 days, continually ask the Holy Spirit to grow your heart for revival and the Church.

INTRODUCTION

O ne of the more disturbing verses in Scripture concerns the second man to ever live, Cain, the eldest son of Adam and Eve. After killing his brother, Abel, Cain is put under a curse and becomes a wanderer. The ground, which received his brother Abel's blood, will no longer produce for Cain. Cain, a worker of the soil, is cut-off from his means of livelihood by his own actions. Following his conversation with God after Abel's murder, comes an action that foreshadows much of future human history. It is found in Genesis 4:16. *"So Cain went out from the Lord's presence and lived in the land of Nod, east of Eden."*

We don't know where Nod was. There is no recollection in any historical account of where this land was. But the Hebrew meaning of the word "nod" tells us much about the spiritual condition of Cain. Nod means "wanderings" in the original Hebrew. Cain went out into the land of wanderings—wanderings apart from the presence of God.

We don't know if Cain had a choice here. Maybe he was driven from the Lord's presence, though the text does not clearly state that. It seems more likely that Cain chose to leave the Lord's presence because of his sin and feelings of guilt. It certainly seems that way when you consider the resultant generations and their wickedness and rebellion against God.

What Cain did physically, mankind since has done spiritually. We have left the presence of the Lord. Wandering off in our ways, doing what seems right to us. Ignoring our Maker, we live in the land of Nod.

It is easy to understand how those who have never encountered the grace and mercy of God through Jesus Christ can wander off. It is almost beyond belief that Christians can do the same. But I would suggest to you, with sorrow, that much of the Church today is asleep in the land of Nod. They have left the presence of God for a life of wandering apart from Him.

Harsh words? Perhaps! But consider the warnings of Scripture about just such a possibility. Jesus asked if He would find faith on earth when He returned. The Apostle John in the letters to the seven churches in the Book of Revelation warns about the danger of a church failing to remain a church. The author of Hebrews warns against the danger of drifting away from the faith.

Perhaps that phrase "drifting away" may be helpful to us as we try to understand the dangers here. We may not be like Cain and simply leave God's presence. It may be more of a drifting away. Less time with Him today—even less time tomorrow. Suddenly it seems we are so far away that it might not be worth the effort to try and return.

Have you ever been in a rowboat on a good-sized lake? The boat isn't far from shore, and it wouldn't take long to row back to the dock. But the sun is hot and feels so good as it beats down on you that you decide to close your eyes and take a bit of a nap. You awake from your nap, astonished at how far away the dock is now. It's no longer a short row, but a long distance requiring strenuous effort. You didn't so much decide to leave the shore as you simply decided to let things drift. This is what Hebrews warns us against.

The third verse of the old hymn, "Come, Thou Fount of Every Blessing" speaks much to us of this tendency toward drifting.

O to grace how great a debtor, Daily I'm constrained to be!
Let Thy goodness, like a fetter, Bind my wandering heart to Thee:
Prone to wander, Lord, I feel it, Prone to leave the God I love:
Here's my heart, O take and seal it; Seal it for Thy courts above.

This leaving the presence of the Lord can obviously happen to an individual, but it is of great concern that it can happen to a body of believers as well. The Lord's warning to the Ephesian Church in the second chapter of Revelation is directed at the whole congregation. Together they had served the Lord and held on to the right doctrines, but had lost their first love. As a church, they had left the Lord's presence and were dwelling in the land of Nod.

How many congregations today are asleep in the land of Nod? Isn't it interesting that there are outward similarities in the Hebrew word for wanderings (nod) and our English word "nod." Webster's dictionary defines the English word "nod" as, "a quick downward motion of the head as one falls off to sleep." Sleepy churches, drifting off to sleep, moving away from the presence of God, not so much by intention, as by inaction.

These spiritually sleepy churches may be very noisy, filled with loud songs and much activity. But in fact a spiritual drowsiness has come over them as they drift away from any true interaction with the Christ who is their Head.

What will wake up sleepy Christians in the land of Nod? Only a fresh awakening to the presence of Christ in their midst! This is not a call to a new program for waking the sleeping. Enough of our programs! It is a call for repentance and a return to the presence of Christ. It is a call for *revival!*

This revival will happen as pastors and church leaders lead their congregations in prayers of humility and repentance for trying to do the Lord's work apart from His strength and empowerment. It will happen as preachers covenant to preach Christ and Him alone. It will happen as individual believers resolve to seek His face in a fresh, new way. It will happen as our hearts join with the heart of David as he prays, *"My heart says of you, 'Seek his face!' Your face Lord, I will seek"* (Psalm 27:8).

DAY ONE

"Restore us again, O God our Savior, and put away your displeasure toward us. Will you be angry with us forever? Will you prolong your anger through all generations? Will you not revive us again, that your people may rejoice in you?"
(Psalm 85:4-6)

Most of us are afraid of the wrong things. We worry about what people think of us. Or we fear cancer or other deadly diseases. Maybe it's the state of the economy or the moral slide in our culture? Perhaps what we should fear is a God who is angry with us?

The fear of God is not a popular topic today. Most would rather hear about the love of God, and in many ways, that is good. Nothing is more important than the love of God. But we can never adequately understand the love of God apart from the fear of God.

Ancient Israel understood that God's anger over their sin was a block to their receiving the benefits of His love. The solution to their national and spiritual condition was to deal with the displeasure of God so that they could be restored in His sight. The Church today must face this same issue. There is a Divine, holy anger over sin and rebellion that cannot be ignored. What we really need is revival!

Christians around the world are praying for revival. What are they praying for and do they have good reason to expect revival? Is revival something God wants to do for His people today? To answer these questions, we need to understand that God has always worked in the area of revival with His people. Revival is

God's pattern. From the earliest days of Israel, on through the history of the Church, God's method of dealing with His people has been to grant periodic times of special blessing in which His presence is made manifest and His people are drawn back to Him. The result of that is a changed society.

Perhaps the clearest view of revival can be seen by examining Israel's past. Historians tell us that there are seven major revivals in the Old Testament. I would suggest that if you take away the word "major" there are somewhere between fifteen and sixteen revivals. These were very clear, distinct times, in which the people of God were restored to a time of religious excitement, enthusiasm, and commitment with a resultant change in society.

Prayer Focus: Pray that the Lord would teach you much about His heart for revival in our day.

Prayer: Lord, I have so much to learn about revival. Please teach me what You want me to know.

Next Step: I know we don't like to focus on the anger of God, but to bring this issue home, would you think about one area of your life that displeases God. I'm sure there is more than one, but just focus on one area. Bring it before the Lord in repentance and ask for forgiveness and restoration in this area.

Lord, what area in my life displeases you? Abide. Teach me to abide in you daily, hourly, minute by minute. Faith - give me the faith to trust you.

obey - by your Spirit cause me to walk out your commands in obedien

DAY TWO

"Then his people recalled the days of old, the days of Moses and his people— where is he who brought them through the sea, with the shepherd of his flock? Where is he who set his Holy Spirit among them?" (Isaiah 63:11)

The older I get, the more important memories become. Certainly additional years add up the number of memories, but it's more than that. Memories have a way of bringing back a moment in the past and infusing it with new life and transforming the present. That's why Scripture so often commands the people of God to "remember." Isaiah speaks of a time when the people recalled a past move of God.

As we look at God's pattern of revival, we typically see something like this: Israel, as a people, was called by God to make a difference, called to be a light to the Gentiles. You see them under leaders such as Moses or David, who are living a life that causes them to be set apart from the people around them. The people are worshipping God, holding on to His Word, doing what God wants them to do. Then, typically, a generation or so after the leader has died, you see Israel begin to slide. You see them move farther and farther away from obedience to the Word of God. They begin to accept idolatry from the tribes around them. Pagan practices begin to come in, with acts of immorality and all the problems associated with that. Eventually come times of war and even slavery.

Typically at this point of decline there arises a remnant of people who begin to pray. They begin to cry out to God asking the Lord to save them. Then, in His own timing, God sends a leader and there comes a time of revival when they begin to throw off their idolatry and paganism and restore once again the true worship of Jehovah. They begin to again hold on to the Word of God. The nation experiences a time of national prosperity, spiritual excitement and religious significance that lasts for about a generation. Then you see the cycle begin to happen again. Over and over again throughout the Old Testament: revival and decline, revival and decline.

Where are we today in this pattern? To make it even more personal, where are you? Are you in a time of revival or decline? Our spiritual lives are not set in concrete. There are times of great excitement, as well as periods of spiritual sleepiness. It is time for us to wake up and experience all that God has for us in Christ Jesus!

Prayer Focus: Ask the Lord to reveal to the Church today where we are in the cycle of revival and decline. Help us to see with clarity the need of the hour.

Prayer: Help me Lord, to be like the men of Issachar in the Old Testament, who understood the times in which they lived and knew what Israel must do.

Next Step: Can you clearly remember a time of spiritual excitement and intimacy with Christ in your life? Spend some time relaxing and rejoicing over those memories and ask the Lord to do it again.

DAY THREE

*"Nevertheless, more and more men and women believed in the
Lord and were added to their number." (Acts 5:14)*

As you move into the New Testament you see a group of people
who were born in a time of revival. But we know historically
that it did not last. Through the history of the Church you once
again see the same pattern of revival and decline. It seems to be the
way God deals with His people.

Through the years many countries have experienced periodic
times of revival. Within the United States, we have experienced at
least three times of national revival, known as the Great Awaken-
ings. During these times, God moved and changed the course of
our nation. Many of us believe that God is getting ready to do it
again in our day, in our age.

What is this thing called revival? I believe that revival is the
Church waking up to the presence of Jesus in her midst. It is nothing more and nothing less than you and I beginning to experience
what we already know theologically and intellectually. You believe
that Jesus is with you. Why? Because He said He would be. You
don't necessarily believe it because you feel Him, but just because
Jesus said it. He said that where two or three are gathered together
He too would be in our midst. You also believe Colossians 1:27,
"Christ in us, the hope of glory."

We believe that Jesus is present when we gather as the Church.
But we don't act that way. That is not the way things happen on
Sunday. You know why I know your church needs revival? Because

when church services ended last Sunday, you went home. What would happen if Jesus had been there? Let's just suppose Jesus was there. Would you be looking at your watch? Would you be eager to leave? One characteristic of the great revivals was extended times of worship. They never wanted to end the service. Now obviously people had to leave, they had to take care of physical things, they had jobs to go to, but as soon as they were done, they were back, because that was where God was. They wanted to be in on the action. They wanted to be where God was. They wanted to experience His presence.

I want to suggest to you that revival is not strange or mystical. It is simply the Church waking up to the presence of Christ in her midst. It is almost as though God reaches out and slaps us; and we wake up and we realize God is there. That is what revival is. It is God shaking us. It is God waking us up. And we recognize that Jesus really is here.

What are you doing in your life that attracts the presence of God? Do you have regular times in Scripture and in worship? As you pray, are you seeking His presence, or just what He might give you?

Prayer Focus: Ask the Lord to make you very aware of His presence in your life.

Prayer: Lord Jesus, I know that You are living in me. Help me to be very aware of that awesome fact.

Next Step: As you seek God's presence this week, use the prayer of David in Psalm 27:4, "One thing I ask from the LORD, this only do I seek: that I may dwell in the house of the LORD all the days of my life, to gaze on the beauty of the LORD and to seek him in his temple."

DAY FOUR

"Repent, then, and turn to God, so that your sins may be wiped out, that times of refreshing may come from the Lord."
(Acts 3:19)

We are desperate for the presence of Jesus in our nation today. I am not in any way a critic of the Church. The more I travel the more I fall in love with the Church of Jesus Christ. I am seeing so many wonderful things happen. Christians are doing wonderful things in the name of Jesus—acts of love, mercy and self-sacrifice. It is amazing what is happening today, and has been happening for years. We are doing all we know to do. But it isn't working.

Most churches have all kinds of activities. They've tried all kinds of programs. They've given and done everything they know how to give and do in order to for the Church to impact society. But even with what has happened in the Church in the United States over the last fifty years, are we a more moral and ethical nation because of what the Church has been doing? It is unbelievable when we consider the tremendous acts of sacrifice, service and ministry in the last fifty years in the Church, and yet it is apparent that the Church is going one way and our nation is moving the opposite way as fast as it can.

In a very real sense, we are at this wonderful point of despair. We are at a wonderful point of hopelessness in which the Church is beginning to recognize that we have been doing everything we know how to do and it is not working. It is time for revival. It is time to humble ourselves before God in prayer and ask Him to make Himself known in the midst of His people so that our nation can be saved and our world impacted for Christ.

What is needed is not bigger buildings or better programs, but more of Jesus! It is the presence of the Lord that will bring revival and indeed, is revival. The Church today must shift its focus off of itself and onto Jesus if we are to see the cultural transformation that we desire.

Prayer Focus: Pray for the Lord to stir many hearts to begin to long for revival.

Prayer: God, would You pour out that godly sense of despair upon us, Your people, that we would turn our hearts to You and would cause us all to trust only in You and Your work in us?

Next Step: What are you doing in your own life to cultivate a desire for the presence of Christ? We don't all develop this in the same way. Perhaps you are one who would profit from quietly reading a great book on revival like Brian Edward's, *Revival! A People Saturated with God.* You might be one who needs to immerse yourself in presence-focused worship music. Whatever fits who you are, this is the time to begin to increase your longing for Him!

DAY FIVE

"To you, LORD, I call; you are my Rock, do not turn a deaf ear to me. For if you remain silent, I will be like those who go down to the pit. Hear my cry for mercy as I call to you for help, as I lift up my hands toward your Most Holy Place."
(Psalm 28:1-2)

Wow does revival come? Any student of revival will tell you that there has never been a revival that was not preceded by a movement of prayer. God always calls His people to prayer in anticipation of revival. I would ask you today to get serious about praying for revival. We need to shift our prayer focus to the issues that are close to God's heart, especially that we, His people, His Church, would wake up and discover the presence of Jesus in our midst.

When that happens, our lives become different. When Jesus is there, things that were acceptable before are no longer acceptable. Some of the things that go on in our church and in our society are changed because it is the Lord who is present.

That is why in those great revivals in the past, there was a bit of emotionalism. Suddenly, people would come into a church service and discover Jesus. Now they did not see Him in the flesh, but there was a powerful sense of the presence of Jesus. What do you suppose happens if you come into a church service during a revival and there is a strong sense of the presence of Jesus and you've been sinning all week? When you come into the presence of the awesome holiness of God suddenly there is weeping, crying out, and sometimes even falling down before God in repentance.

Heaven-sent revival is our only hope. We don't have answers. We don't know what to do. We don't have any programs established in our churches that are changing whole communities and our society. It's just not happening. What we need is God.

How do you pray for revival? Psalm 85 is a good place to begin. "You showed favor to your land, O LORD. You restored the fortunes of Jacob. You forgave the iniquity of your people and covered all their sins. You set aside all your wrath and turned from your fierce anger. Restore us again, O God our Savior, and put away your displeasure toward us. Will you be angry with us forever? Will you prolong your anger through all generations? Will you not revive us again, that your people may rejoice in You?" (vv. 1-6).

Based on that passage we will find ourselves praying, "Lord, revive us again, do it again in our day." We will come before God saying, "Lord, this is what You have done and this is what we want You to do in our life and in our nation."

Prayer Focus: Ask the Lord to do it again in our day. Ask that what He has done in past revivals would be experienced by the Church today.

Prayer: Father, I love hearing about the great revivals of the past. But what we need today is not a history lesson, but a fresh move of Your Spirit in the midst of Your people.

Next Step: What do you think would change in your life if you had a fresh encounter with Jesus? Spend some time meditating and dreaming about what daily life would look like with Jesus close by. You might want to write down the vision of a life of intimacy with Christ.

DAY SIX

*"When Moses came down from Mount Sinai with the two tab-
lets of the covenant law in his hands, he was not aware that his
face was radiant because he had spoken with the Lord"
(Exodus 34:29).*

Though many have given good definitions of revival, I still
like this simple little description: Revival happens when God
shows up for church. In a real sense, the Lord is always present
when His people gather in His name. But all too often His presence
goes unnoticed. This definition recognizes the fact that when the
people of God become aware of the presence of the Lord, everything
changes. Our worship services, our family lives, our evangelistic
efforts, and our individual devotional lives will all be different when
God shows up for church.

The Bible teaches us the amazing fact that God has come to
dwell in us through His Holy Spirit. The Old Testament name given
to the Messiah was Emmanuel—God with us. Colossians 1:27
teaches us the mystery of God: "Christ in [us], the hope of glory."
Jesus said, "If anyone loves me, he will obey my teaching. My Father
will love him, and we will come to him and make our home with
him" (John 14:23). The Lord also made it clear that when two or
more of us are gathered together, He would be there in our midst.

Much as the temple or the tabernacle in the Old Testament was
a place where the presence of God was manifest on earth, so now
the gathered Church becomes a place where His presence is known.
Our theology is clear on that fact. Unfortunately, our experience

normally fails to match up to our theology. Most churches meet for worship, teaching and fellowship and leave again without truly being aware of God in their midst.

The presence of God is not something that can be programmed, it can only be desired. Often though, our worship services are centered around too many other things rather than the Lord Himself. We bring good things to the table—edification, encouragement, evangelism—and often forget that which is absolutely essential . . . the presence of God.

Praying for revival is praying for open eyes among the people of God, saying, "Lord, help us to see Jesus! Open the eyes of our hearts that we might know You and become aware of Your presence here in our lives."

Prayer Focus: Ask the Lord to give you open eyes to see and experience all of who He is, for you and the Church.

Prayer: How often Lord, have we sung the little chorus, "Open my eyes Lord, I want to see Jesus" and yet haven't really expected You to do anything? Oh God, today I desperately plead for open spiritual eyes to see You in Your Glory.

Next Step: Could you begin to pray each week for your local church to begin to experience the presence of God? Make this your own prayer project to bring about a dramatic change in your congregational culture by seeking His presence in your assemblies.

DAY SEVEN

*"Then the cloud covered the tent of meeting, and the glory of
the* Lord *filled the tabernacle. Moses could not enter the tent
of meeting because the cloud had settled on it, and the glory of
the* Lord *filled the tabernacle." (Exodus 40:34-35)*

The experience of Israel under the leadership of Moses is a great
example for the Church today as we cry out to God for revival.
My friend, Terry Teykl, has written a powerful book entitled *The
Presence Based Church*. He writes,

> "As a result of their unique relationship with God, the Isra-
> elites became the original Presence-based people. Under the
> leadership of Moses, and at God's bidding, they made the
> Presence the axis of their lives.
> "The Ark of the Covenant was always located in the tab-
> ernacle at the very center of the camp. The 12 tribes were
> divided into four groups and stationed symmetrically around
> the Presence: three to the north, three to the south, three to
> the east, and three to the west. By day they saw the cloud that
> hung over the tent, and by night they would lie in the entrance
> to their own tents and watch the fire. As long as the Presence
> stayed, they stayed. But when the Presence moved, they fol-
> lowed. They were Presence led and Presence drawn" (p. 89).

In Exodus 33:14-17, there is a fascinating conversation between the
Lord and Moses concerning His presence. "The Lord replied, 'My

Presence will go with you, and I will give you rest.' Then Moses said
to him, 'If your Presence does not go with us, do not send us up from
here. How will anyone know that you are pleased with me and with
your people unless you go with us? What else will distinguish me
and your people from all the other people on the face of the earth?'
And the Lord said to Moses, 'I will do the very thing you have asked,
because I am pleased with you and I know you by name.'"

Moses understood how critical it was for Israel to stay with the
presence of God. When the Church today grabs hold of that fact, we
will see revival. When the Church, like Moses, commits to going only
where the Lord leads, then we will be making progress. It is time for
us to cry out for the Lord to make us aware of His presence.

Teykl offers great insight as to the effects of the manifest presence of God.

> "Where His Presence is being manifested, God's glory is
> evident. When the Presence fell on the Mercy Seat of the Ark,
> His glory filled the tabernacle to such an extent that no one
> could go near. His Presence was noticeable. Think about it. If
> God were to manifest His Presence in your church, shouldn't
> it be just as noticeable as it was in the tabernacle? Is not God
> that same God that descended in the Holy Place and rested
> among His chosen people in fire and cloud? Is He not the
> same God who, from the Mercy Seat, displayed His power
> and authority, guided and governed the Israelites, gave them
> victory over their enemies, demonstrated His favor and love,
> established His uniqueness and offered atonement for sin?
> "Where God's Presence is being manifested today, the
> same results are evident. Humility and uncommon zeal char-
> acterize people of the Presence because they have seen His
> power and know of His authority in the earth. Where the
> Presence is, wisdom and peace prevail through His guidance.
> Pathways become clear and sound decisions are made. In

the Presence, people gain victory over habits or emotions that have held them captive for years. Relationships are healed, lives are transformed, joy is evident and the powers of darkness are forced to retreat. In the Presence, many call on the name of Jesus and are saved in response to the wave of supernatural love and grace that penetrates their spirits," (p.201).

Does that sound a bit like revival to you? It does to me. I'm praying for an increased hunger for His presence in my life, my family, and my church. As God answers that prayer, we will begin to see an increased awareness of the activity of the Lord in the midst of His people. Join me in praying for God to "show up for church."

Prayer Focus: Ask the Lord to give you a greater hunger for His presence as you go about each day.

Prayer: Forgive me Lord, when I get hungry for everything except You. Please give me a spiritual hunger that supersedes every other desire.

Next Step: Are there others in your congregation that are also beginning to long for more of God's presence? Schedule a time in one of your homes to pray together about becoming a presence-based Church.

DAY EIGHT

"Help us, O God our Savior, for the glory of your name;
deliver us and forgive our sins for your name's sake."
(Psalm 79:9)

Like a mighty wave rolling across the Church around the world, comes the cry from millions of believers, "Oh God, send a revival!" Like no time in recent history, the Church is becoming aware of its own desperate condition and the even more critical needs of our cultures. It is reassuring to know that for once, the Church is not looking to another program or strategy to try to change the world. We're recognizing that it is going to take heaven-sent revival. Taking our cue from past revivals, the role of revival-praying is moving to the forefront.

What is it we are praying for when we ask God to send revival? To fully answer that would comprise another book, and even that would prove to be inadequate. Christian scholars are even now debating what the nature is of a revival. But praise God, though we disagree on its nature, there is near unanimity on our desperate need for a revival.

Some of my favorite short definitions of revival are as follows:

Revival is "a movement of the Holy Spirit bringing about a revival of New Testament Christianity in the church of Christ and its related community," J. Edwin Orr.

"Revival is a community saturated with God," Duncan Campbell.

"Revival is the Church falling in love with Jesus all over again," Vance Havner.

Perhaps the definition that best fits my own understanding is from Stephen Olford. "Revival is ultimately Christ Himself, seen, felt, heard, living, active, moving in and through His Body on earth."

True revival is not man-centered but Christ-centered. It is not about a type of music or special experience, but a fresh revelation of Christ in the midst of His people . . . a people often grown sleepy or slow-moving and desperately in need of a fresh awakening touch from their Savior.

Prayer Focus: Pray for the Lord to give you a clearer picture of what revival might look like in your church.

Prayer: Help me Lord, to better understand what I am praying for when asking You for revival. Give me insight into those passages of Scripture that show how You moved with power among Your people.

Next Step: Write your own definition of revival. It doesn't have to sound like previous definitions. If it's truly yours, it will help you as you prayer toward the fulfillment of that vision.

DAY NINE

"Teach me your way, LORD, that I may rely on your faithfulness; give me an undivided heart, that I may fear your name. I will praise, Lord my God, with all my heart; I will glorify your name forever." (Psalm 86:11-12)

Much has been written on what happens when revival touches a church, community or nation. But foundational to each of those spheres of revival is a fresh touch from Christ upon an individual. J. Edwin Orr speaks of those different spheres this way: "Such an awakening may change in a significant way an individual; or it may affect a larger group of believers; or it may move a congregation or the churches in the city or district, or the body of believers throughout a country or continent; or indeed the larger body of believers throughout the world."

What would it mean for an individual to experience revival? It is an important question for us to consider. Though we may long for and pray for revival for the whole Church, we certainly want to make sure that we as individuals are a part of that revival. Can revival perhaps come to an individual apart from the corporate aspect? Dare we begin to ask God for revival in our own lives?

I believe there is a very clear correlation between what happens when a church experiences revival and when an individual Christian experiences revival. The heart of revival is when Christ shows up for church. It is when we begin to experience what we already know is true biblically and theologically concerning the presence of Christ. One of the major tenets of our faith is that when believers in Jesus gather, He Himself is present in a very special way in their midst. Jesus said, "when two of you gather in my name, I am there in your midst" (Matthew 18:20). We believe His words concerning His presence as we gather. Yet Sunday after Sunday, in the majority of our churches, we go through the motions without a real awareness of Jesus actually being there with us. In revival, there is an awakening to His presence. Biblical truths that had perhaps grown stale are suddenly infused with new life. The love and life of Jesus are lived out in fresh new ways as the Church gathers.

Prayer Focus: Bring before the Lord your own congregation, asking Him to bring a fresh awareness of His presence in your assemblies.

Prayer: May we never again, Lord, assemble in Your name without experiencing Your presence. Help us to linger as long as it takes for us to wake up to who You are in our midst.

Next Step: Write out a personal prayer of presence. Make it a short invitation to the Lord to "show up," whether in your own life personally or in your congregation. Put this written prayer in multiple places where you will see it through the day and always remember to pray.

DAY TEN

"To them God has chosen to make known among the Gentiles the glorious riches of this mystery, which is Christ in you, the hope of glory." (Colossians 1:27)

Personal or individual revival should not be something just for the super spiritual. It's really very simple and should be the mark of every day Christian life. Paul made it clear to the Colossians and to us as he described our life as that of the indwelling Christ. Colossians 1:27 speaks to us of, "Christ in us, the hope of glory." Is there a more astonishing verse in Scripture? That the Son of God has actually come to take up residence within the individual Christian? Yet we often view such a verse as dry biblical truth. It somehow fails to excite or thrill the soul. Even more telling, it fails to change the way we live.

What a difference it would make in our lives if we truly lived out the truth of Christ in us, the hope of glory. As we walk daily with Jesus, we become aware of His presence, His love, His strength, and His direction. We often abstractly ask ourselves, "What would Jesus do?" But what changes would occur if we directly asked our indwelling Lord, "Jesus, what are You doing?" What a revival of changed life, character, and witness we would see among believers.

The 19th century Quaker author, Hannah Whitall Smith writes,

> "Dear friend, I make the glad announcement to thee that the Lord is in thy heart. Since the day of thy conversion He has been dwelling there, but thou hast lived on in ignorance of

it. Every moment during all that time might have been passed in the sunshine of His sweet presence, and every step have been taken under His advice. But because thou knew it not, and did not look for Him there, thy life has been lonely and full of failure. But now that I make the announcement to thee, how wilt thou receive it? Art thou glad to have Him? Wilt thou throw wide open every door to welcome Him in? Wilt thou joyfully and thankfully give up the government of thy life into His hands? Wilt thou consult Him about everything, and let Him decide each step for thee, and mark out every path? Wilt thou invite Him into thy innermost chambers, and make Him the sharer in thy most hidden life? Wilt thou say 'Yes' to all His longing for union with thee, and with a glad and eager abandonment hand thyself and all that concerns thee over into His hands? If thou wilt, then shall thy soul begin to know something of the joy of union with Christ."

If revival is experiencing the presence of Christ in a fresh new way, then this certainly is a description of the revived life. It is a life that points to Jesus and in fact, draws many to the life of Jesus being lived out in the believer.

Prayer Focus: Pray that today, the reality of the Lord's presence in your life would be more real than life itself.

Prayer: Lord Jesus, please live out Your life fully in me today. Do all that You desire in and through me.

Next Step: Here is an exercise of the imagination. You and Moses are having a conversation. Try to explain to this Old Testament saint how the Creator of the universe has come to dwell within you. Imagine his response as he tries to comprehend the Holy One of Israel coming to dwell in human flesh.

DAY ELEVEN

"But you are a chosen people, a royal priesthood,
a holy nation, God's special possession, that you may declare
the praises of him who called you out of darkness into
his wonderful light." (1 Peter 2:9)

On a practical level, how can we begin to walk in this intimate relationship with Jesus? Years ago I heard Argentinian evangelist Juan Carlos Ortiz say, "to walk in the Spirit is to be continually conscious of Christ in you." One of the major goals of my life has been to narrow the gaps of unawareness. It is so easy to get caught up in daily life, even in service to Jesus, and forget the awesome fact of the indwelling Christ. To combat that, we need to put up markers in our daily life to remind us of this astonishing fact. I remember hearing one preacher tell of how, upon entering his car, he would push aside the books that were on the car seat and then invite the Lord to scoot over close to him. He knew that Jesus, being in the Spirit, did not need a place to sit, but the imagery helped remind this man of the Lord's presence with him. We would all profit much from building such reminders into daily life.

Scriptures are so clear that our lives are hidden with Christ, we are seated with Christ, we are to follow Him. Paul went so far as to say, "It is no longer I who live, but Christ living in me" (see Galatians 2:20). True spiritual awakening begins on a personal basis as we begin to live out daily the truth of God's Word, "Christ in us, the hope of glory."

Prayer Focus: Today, ask the Lord to bring reminders into our lives of the life of Jesus being lived out in us.

Prayer: I ask You, Lord, to keep reminding me today that You are not far away, but near. Please do whatever it takes to keep truth in the forefront of my mind and experience.

Next Step: Our biggest problem with this teaching is unawareness of the indwelling Christ. Can you set up markers or reminders for yourself throughout the day to make you aware of His presence? Perhaps your meals can remind you that he is the bread of life. Maybe sitting behind the wheel of a car can stir you to remembrance that it is Jesus who really moves you throughout life. Find something that works for you.

DAY TWELVE

"Then the angel said to me, 'Write this: Blessed are those who are invited to the wedding supper of the Lamb!' And he added, 'These are the true words of God.'" (Revelation 19:9)

As a minister of the gospel, I have officiated at many weddings. There are so many details to be attended to. Guests must be seated, candles lit, songs played, aisle runners in place. But the most essential detail is this: Is the bride ready? Until she is ready and in place, the wedding cannot begin, no matter how many other details have been taken care of.

The Lord has been working on me lately about the preparation of the Bride of Christ for her wedding day. Scripture is clear in its presentation of the Church as the Bride of Christ. Revelation 19:7-8 is a beautiful picture of this couple and their wedding day. "Let us rejoice and be glad and give him glory! For the wedding of the Lamb has come, and his bride has made herself ready. Fine linen, bright and clean, was given her to wear. (Fine linen stands for the righteous acts of the saints.)"

Actually, the idea of the Lord being married to His people is not unique to the New Testament. The Old Testament writers often referred to Israel as a bride, pledged to be married to the Lord, the Bridegroom. Isaiah writes, "as a bridegroom rejoices over his bride, so will your God rejoice over you" (Isaiah 62:5). Jeremiah continues this imagery: "I remember the devotion of your youth, how as a bride you loved me and followed me through the desert, through a land not sown. . . . Does a maiden forget her jewelry, a bride her wedding ornaments? Yet my people have forgotten me, days without number" (Jeremiah 2:2, 32).

How could God express in any better way His desire for intimacy with His people than to use the illustration of a man and women who court and then are betrothed to one another, finally resulting in a wedding and the consummation of their union? Throughout Scripture, this is God's expressed desire and ultimate purpose for His people.

As I have been studying the Scriptures that relate to this powerful picture of the Lord and His people, I've become increasingly aware of the need to prepare the Bride for her wedding day. As we move closer to the day of the Lord's return, this becomes an increasingly urgent task. Referring again to Revelation 19:7, two things are indicated about the preparation of the Bride. First, she will be ready for the wedding. Secondly, she herself is the one who will make the preparations for the wedding. "For the wedding of the Lamb has come, and his bride has made herself ready."

Without being critical, does it seem to you that the Church, the Bride of Christ is ready for the wedding? If not, then it is time to bear down and concentrate on this preparatory work. It is time to prepare the Bride for her wedding day!

Prayer Focus: Ask the Lord to teach you ways in which the Church must begin to prepare herself for the return of the Bridegroom, Jesus Christ.

Prayer: Father, would You so touch the heart of the Church with love for Your Son Jesus that we find ourselves eagerly preparing ourselves for the great wedding feast of the Lamb?

Next Step: If you knew you had one month to live, what would you do to prepare yourself to meet the Lord? Write it down. In all probability, that month of preparation would be a month of revival. What from that list can you begin to do today?

DAY THIRTEEN

"How priceless is your unfailing love, O God! People take refuge in the shadow of your wings. They feast on the abundance of your house: you give them drink from your river of delights. For with you is the fountain of life: in your light we see light. Continue your love to those who know you, your righteousness to the upright in heart." (Psalm 36:8-10)

What does it mean for the Bride to be prepared to meet the Bridegroom? The first truth that is a key to preparation is the issue of ownership or belonging. In John 3:29 we read, "The bride belongs to the bridegroom." Most cultures today are not comfortable with the idea of the marriage relationship being one of ownership of one person by another. But we do understand what it means to belong to someone. There is not just a legal connection, but a passionate, emotional attachment.

The Church, as the Bride of Christ, belongs to Jesus. It is not only a legal issue accomplished at Calvary, but it is also a matter of the heart. It is a love relationship in which no other love or desire may enter to mar or damage the relationship. I remember singing the hymn, "Now I Belong to Jesus," many times as I was growing up. It is time for the Church to realize that we belong to Him and begin to nurture that love relationship.

Another truth about preparation of the Bride of Christ is found in Peter's 2nd Epistle as he teaches about the Second Coming of Christ. He writes, "So then, dear friends, since you are looking for-

ward to this, make every effort to be found spotless, blameless and
at peace with him" (3:14). Peter gives us these very practical areas
of preparation for the wedding of Christ and His people. This passage is one of the reasons I believe a great revival is coming for the
Church. A revived Church is one that is consciously turning from
sin in repentance and longing to be found spotless and blameless.
A revived Church has submitted to the Lordship and Authority of
Christ and will be at peace with her Bridegroom.

The Apostle John saw a vision of a prepared Bride. "I saw the
Holy City, the new Jerusalem, coming down out of heaven from
God, prepared as a bride beautifully dressed for her husband" (Rev-
elation 21:2). Is that a passion of your life? Are you committed to
seeing the Church prepared for the Coming of her Bridegroom, the
Lord Jesus?

As I prayed and studied over this topic, I was taught a hard
lesson by the Lord. In the midst of a prayer time, I pictured in
my mind's eye a bride standing at the altar, waiting for the bridegroom. But as I continued in prayer, there came one of those sacred
moments in which the Lord placed a thought in my mind and made
the simple statement: "The Bride is not at the altar yet."

That is a simple statement of fact, yet also a rebuke and an
encouragement. The Church, the Bride, is not at the altar waiting
for the Bridegroom. The Bride is off doing a multitude of things,
but very little of it concerns waiting at the altar for her Beloved. The
rebuke was clear, but so was the encouragement.

It is time to bring the Bride to the altar. It is time for the Church
to become a house of prayer. The kneeling Church becomes the
Bride at the altar, prepared for the Bridegroom. "The Spirit and the
bride say, 'Come'" (Revelation 22:17)!

Prayer Focus: Pray that the Church would set aside lesser things and begin to
focus passionately upon Jesus Christ as we eagerly anticipate His return for us.

Prayer: Lord, help me not to get so caught up in the busy affairs of this life that I forget to look up in anticipation of Your return.

Next Step: What do you believe needs to happen in order for the Bride of Christ to be ready for the Bridegroom? You can consider the whole Church as a part of your answer, but don't forget to consider your own checklist. How can you personally be more prepared for the Coming of Christ?

DAY FOURTEEN

"Therefore, because of you the heavens have withheld their dew and the earth its crops." (Haggai 1:10)

In every society, in every land, and in every age, rain is important. We depend upon it as a source of life. Without rain our crops die, gardens wither, grass turns brown, and our water supplies begin to dry up. We must have rain to have life.

There are spiritual droughts as well. They come upon individuals, churches, and nations. They come as seasons of spiritual dryness when apathy, inactivity, and sin characterize our lives. God's Word speaks clearly to us about these times of spiritual drought.

"God sets the lonely in families, he leads forth the prisoners with singing; but the rebellious live in a sun-scorched land." (Psalm 68:6)
"You will be like an oak with fading leaves, like a garden without water." (Isaiah 1:30)
"The poor and needy search for water, but there is none; their tongues are parched with thirst." (Isaiah 41:17)
"O God, you are my God; earnestly I seek you; my soul thirsts for you, my body longs for you, in a dry and weary land where there is no water." (Psalm 63:1)

I believe these verses describe much of the world today, a dry and weary land where there is no water. It might describe you as an individual as well. Is there a spiritual dryness in your life? Is there a lack of enthusiasm and excitement concerning spiritual matters? Is your prayer life dull or virtually non-existent? Hold on—the rain is coming!

Prayer Focus: Ask the Lord to help you deal with spiritual dryness in your life.

Prayer: O God, I thirst for the living water that is You. Help me to not be satisfied with anything less than You, Yourself.

Next Step: Sit down at a table and set before you a big empty glass. Stare at its emptiness and find yourself getting thirsty. Now fill it up with cold, pure water. Have a drink. Thank God for good water. Then thank Him for the living water that He has poured into your life.

DAY FIFTEEN

*"Everyone who drinks this water will be thirsty again, but
whoever drinks the water I give them will never thirst. Indeed,
the water I give them will become in them a spring of water
welling up to eternal life." (John 4:13-14)*

Scriptures do not only speak of these times of spiritual dryness,
they also speak of times of refreshing, of rain from heaven.

"Let my teaching fall like rain and my words descend like
dew, like showers on new grass, like abundant rain on new
plants." (Deuteronomy 32:2)
"He will be like rain falling on a mown field, like showers
watering the earth." (Psalm 72:6)
"I will bless them and the places surrounding my hill. I will
send down showers in season; there will be showers of blessing." (Ezekiel 34:26)
"Let us acknowledge the LORD; let us press on to acknowledge him. As surely as the sun rises, he will appear; he will
come to us like the winter rains, like the spring rains that
water the earth." (Hosea 6:3)
"Sow for yourselves righteousness, reap the fruit of unfailing love, and break up your fallow ground; for it is time to
seek the LORD, until he comes and showers righteousness on
you." (Hosea 10:12)

What is this rain we so long for and need? Ultimately, it is the

Lord's presence. Jesus Himself spoke of the living water that we would need in our lives. The times of refreshing that Scripture speaks of is not so much an experience as it is a Person. It is waking up to the presence of Christ in our lives.

Prayer Focus: Ask the Lord for a downpour of His presence in your life, making you continually aware of His work in you.

Prayer: Lord, may Your Holy Spirit well up within me as that river of living water. Please flow from my life and bring life to everyone and everything that is touched.

Next Step: It's time to get wet. The next time it rains in your area (and that will vary greatly), go out and stand in the rain. If you are a bit health fragile, take your umbrella. If healthy, then just enjoy getting wet. Make this a very special prayer of thanksgiving, not only for the physical rain around you, but for the rain of the Spirit that brings life.

DAY SIXTEEN

"But seek first his kingdom and his righteousness, and all these things will be given to you as well." (Matthew 6:33)

Whether we are asking for ourselves, our church, or our nation, Hosea 10:12 gives us what we need to do to end drought and prepare for rain.

"Sow for yourselves righteousness." Both Old and New Testaments teach us the spiritual principles that you reap what you sow. If you plant wheat, you do not harvest corn. If you plant immorality, you will harvest immorality. Much of the world has been sowing greed, pleasure, immorality, and self-centeredness, and we are reaping the results of that. Unfortunately, it is all too easy for the Church to join with society in reaping the same damaging harvest. God's Word says to sow righteousness, to sow right things. We must speak right things, watch right things, read right things, and do right things. The Bible becomes the means for us to see what those right things are. God's Word gives us a standard for righteousness. Righteousness is not what seems right to a man, but what is right to God.

"Reap the fruit of unfailing love." When righteousness has been sown, we will begin to harvest the fruit of unfailing love. God loves everyone, but the fruit, the benefits of that love, come to those who are moving to establish God's righteousness as the standard for their lives. There are many unclaimed blessings. One of the most neglected is the fruit of unfailing love. It only comes to those who have sown righteousness in their lives.

"Break up your unplowed ground" Unplowed ground has a hard

time receiving rain. Sun-scorched, baked earth forms a hard crust and when rain comes, it simply runs off rather than soak in and make a difference. Unplowed ground is a picture of the unrepentant life. The rain of God's righteousness will not soak in and change a life that is hard and unrepentant. So the command here is this: "Repent! Change! Go a different direction!" That is always God's call to those seeking revival. Today, so many seeking revival—the rain from heaven—seem to want just good feelings or nice meetings. However, the good things of revival come only after times of tears and repentance. God's command is to break up the hard, unplowed ground of your lives before you will see the rain of revival.

"It is time to seek the Lord." Those who are in periods of spiritual dryness often go looking for answers in many places. But God's Word directs us to seek the Lord, for he is the only source for the renewing rain of heaven. You may argue, "But I'm already a Christian. Why should I seek the Lord?"

The sad truth is that we all have a tendency to move away from His presence. We find ourselves spiritually dry and wonder why such a thing could happen to a believer. The Lord's presence must be continually sought after. Complacency and a natural tendency toward getting distracted by the affairs of this world require us again and again to put aside other matters so that we may seek after the Lord. Whenever there is spiritual drought in the land and rain is being desired, the almost automatic response ought to be, "It is time to seek the Lord!" Seeking requires effort. It is not a vague desire but a consuming passion. It requires persevering prayer. Though times of regional or national revival are completely in the Lord's hands, personal revival and renewal comes when we commit ourselves to seek the Lord.

Hosea 10:12 gives great hope to us today. When we have broken up the unplowed ground in repentance and begin to seek the Lord with all our heart, then the promise comes. It is the Lord Himself who comes in response to a repentant, seeking heart—ready to shower His righteousness upon us. It is Jesus, Himself, in the midst of His people, receiving our worship, and showering upon us the blessings of His presence.

Prayer Focus: Ask the Lord to prepare your heart for revival, doing a deep work in you even in the midst of everyday life.

Prayer: Lord, would You increase my desire for You until it becomes an overwhelming passion in my life?

Next Step: Have you experienced a time of spiritual dryness in your life? What do you believe caused that? How did you come out of that time (if you have)? Is the picture of unplowed ground a good one for you to consider for both now and the future?

DAY SEVENTEEN

"Go, consecrate the people. Tell them, 'Consecrate yourselves in preparation for tomorrow; for this is what the LORD, the God of Israel, says: There are devoted things among you, Israel. You cannot stand against your enemies until you remove them.'" (Joshua 7:13)

Christians around the world are longing for and praying for revival. Most of us understand, at some level, that our own sin indicates the need for revival, but may also be that which is blocking the coming of revival. Looking to past revivals for guidance, it seems that without repentance, there may be no expectation of revival. It becomes imperative that we learn how to deal with our own sin.

Dealing with personal sin is something that should be taught at a very early stage in our Christian life. Sin is a reality that we must learn to deal with. The Apostle John tells us that, "If we claim to be without sin, we deceive ourselves" (1 John.1:8). The question then becomes, "How do we deal with personal sin?"

It seems there are two extremes. One is to ignore sin. That seems to be prevalent even in the Church today. We lose sight of the call to holiness and what it means to follow Jesus. The other extreme is to be afraid that every time you sin you've lost your salvation. There are those who live in such a state of fear that they can hardly function as Christians.

The biblical way to deal with personal sin is perhaps best found in Psalm 51. This psalm is prayed and written right after David has been exposed as an adulterer and murderer. We can learn from

David the proper reaction to personal sin.

There must first be an acknowledgment of sin. Until we accept the fact that there is sin in our life, there can be no confession, forgiveness, and restoration. Confession is basically agreeing with God that what we have done is sin. In Psalm 51:4, David makes the important step of realizing that sin is an affront to God Himself. "Against you, you only, have I sinned and done what is evil in your sight." In understanding this fact, sorrow for sin becomes real and leads to further steps.

As David begins to understand the sinfulness of his actions, he expresses his desire for cleansing and forgiveness. In his eagerness to receive forgiveness he uses a variety of terms: "have mercy," "blot out," "wash away," and "cleanse." It all comes down to asking God for forgiveness. The promise of Scripture is that God will forgive. It is important for Christians to memorize and believe with all their hearts the truth of 1 John 1:9: "If we confess our sins, he is faithful and just and will forgive us our sins and purify us from all unrighteousness."

Prayer Focus: Ask the Lord to reveal any sin in you that is preventing you from experiencing all that God has in store for you.

Prayer: My Father, I am so grateful that You are faithful even when I am not. Thank You for not allowing me to stay in my sin. Please continue to reveal any sin or iniquity in my life that I may turn from that sin and back to You.

Next Step: Have you followed the process of Psalm 51 in dealing with sin? Perhaps one of the best ways is to read it again and then write down the principles that David used in coming before the Lord with his sin. Keep those notes handy. You'll need them!

DAY EIGHTEEN

"For he chose us in him before the creation of the world to be
holy and blameless in his sight." (Ephesians 1:4)

True repentance never stays merely at the stage of confessing sin
and desiring forgiveness. It moves us beyond that to a desire
for a pure heart. There comes a longing to stay out of sin, to walk in
victory. It is crying out, "O God, don't let me do this again!" David
prayed it this way: "Create in me a pure heart, O God, and renew a
steadfast spirit within me" (Psalm 51:10). In asking for a new heart,
we realize the need for sanctification, the power not to sin.

We will sin. But our desire has changed. We no longer desire sin.
In fact, we have come to hate sin, especially our own. Our desire is
now for purity and holiness. If that desire is not in you, you've never
fully dealt with sin in your life. All too many Christians short-cir-
cuit the process of repentance and stop before they get to this point.

What happens in us after we have gone through this process of
confession and repentance? David's response to forgiveness was to experience a restoration of joy and praise. "Restore to me the joy of your
salvation and grant me a willing spirit, to sustain me" (51:12), and "O
Lord, open my lips, and my mouth will declare your praise" (51:15).

God's people are a worshipping people. They are a forgiven people who have something to shout about, who have a reason for joy.
Peter writes, "But you are a chosen people, a royal priesthood, a holy
nation, a people belonging to God that you may declare the praises
of him who called you out of darkness into his wonderful light" (1
Peter 2:9). Praise is what forgiven people do!

David goes beyond worship in his response to the forgiveness of God. David did not keep what God had done bottled up inside him. He had been forgiven and he wanted the world to know it. He declares, "Then I will teach transgressors your ways, and sinners will turn back to you" (Psalm 51:13.) If we are going to be effective in sharing the gospel, it's going to be because we really believe that God has done something tremendous in our lives and we want that to happen in the lives of others, too.

How do you deal with sin in your life? God has provided the answer to your sins in the person of Jesus. He doesn't want a single one of us to walk around burdened by sin. Perhaps right now is the time to bring your sins to the only One who can deal with them. Church attendance won't cleanse you from sin. Ministry and acts of service won't cover your sin. Only Jesus can do that. God is calling the Church to repentance! Turn from sin! Agree with God about the sinfulness of your sin. Ask for forgiveness. Trust in the cleansing blood of Jesus to provide not only forgiveness, but the power to avoid sin in the future. Begin today to sing the praises of the One who has washed you and made you clean forever.

"Repent, then, and turn to God, so that your sins may be wiped out, that times of refreshing may come from the Lord" (Acts 3:19).

Prayer Focus: Allow the Lord's amazing grace and forgiveness to wash over you, resulting in prayers of worship and praise.

Prayer: Lord, help me to see sin as You see sin. I want to walk in ways that please You always. Thank You for providing the power to walk with You through the blood of Jesus.

Next Step: Analyze your sin-tolerance. Have you learned to hate sin? One of the ways you can tell is if you are now more sensitive to sin than you were when you were younger. Many have told how movies they had watched in their early walk with the Lord now seemed unattractive to them. They had lost the desire for entertainment that was questionable in nature. Have you noticed a greater desire for holiness in your life?

DAY NINETEEN

"I confess my iniquity; I am troubled by my sin."

(Psalm 38:18)

There is a tendency for us to think of confession as a personal act we do before God. Certainly much confession is of this personal, private nature that is between only God and ourselves. But God's Word gives us another picture of confession that is corporate in its practice. It is confession from a group of people who are aware of the corporate aspect of their sin and aware that private confession is inadequate to deal with this problem.

I believe that the call of God to the Church today is for confession of this type. If we are to see revival in our day, it will come to a people who have humbled themselves together before their God and sought His face. This humility comes as we recognize that much of what has passed for Christianity in our day has been self-centered, worldly, and is an affront to the Lord. The only way to deal with the sin of the Church is for the Church to confess its sins and repent.

The biblical example that comes to mind is the story of Israel during the time of Ezra, when the people of God were dealing with the sin of intermarriage with pagan tribes around them. The seventy years of exile in Babylon had ended. The exiles returned to Jerusalem over a number of years in different groups. One of these groups was lead by the great biblical scholar and man of God, Ezra.

Ezra's godly presence prompts the people to confess that they had once again damaged Israel's standing with God by disobeying His clear command to not intermarry with the non-Jewish peoples around them. The sorrow and prayer of Ezra following this revelation is powerful. As you read Ezra 9:1-10:4, notice several points that we need to bring into our own lives.

- Ezra identified with the sins of the people. Even though he himself had not committed this sin, he prays about "our sin."
- Ezra (and his people) had a great sorrow over this sin. He would pray, "I am too ashamed and disgraced to lift up my face" (9:6).
- Ezra based his awareness of sin on Scripture, not just his own tradition. He literally quoted Scripture back to God in his prayer to demonstrate his awareness of the gravity of the rebellion that had taken place.
- He affirms the righteousness and mercy of God. He even tells God, "You have punished us less than our sins have deserved" (9:13).
- Following the prayer of repentance and confession, there is action taken to make right the situation. It was a hard choice for many. Families were torn apart in order to bring the nation back into right alignment with the Word of God. This was not mere religious talk, but hard action in obeying God.

This is true confession and repentance. The people of God stood convicted of their sin by the Word of God. In sorrow and humility, they bowed before God in prayer and in action. God heard their prayers and restored their nation.

Will we have the courage of their prayers and deeds? Will the Church of Jesus Christ in our day rise up in horror at our acceptance of the standards and moral laxity of our society within the Church itself? Will we see an Ezra arise to call us back to the Word of God?

Prayer Focus: Ask the Lord to allow you to walk in repentance, not as a one time act, but as a way of life.

Prayer: God, send a spirit of repentance upon Your people. Help us to accept the judgment of Your Word in our lives and assemblies. May we walk in that humility that continually confesses that You alone are righteous. Give us the courage to stand together as Your people in confession and repentance, that we might experience a fresh sense of Your Presence in our midst.

Next Step: Have you ever confessed sins that you personally have not committed? Spend some prayerful time considering your own congregation and some of the sins that characterize your assembly. Confess those sins before the Lord. After all, you really are part of the same family and those sins affect you as well as though who are engaged in those sins.

DAY TWENT Y

*"Blessed are those who keep his statutes and seek him with
all their hearts" (Psalm 119:2).*

I'm convinced that one of the greatest problems facing the Church
today is disobedience to God's Word. Among evangelicals at
least, there is a firm commitment to the authority of the Bible.
That's not the problem. We believe the Bible is God's Word. Our
difficulty is in doing what it says. We have Bible studies in all of our
churches, but are we doing what the Bible says?

James gives us the clear command in James 1:22 "Do not merely
listen to the Word, and so deceive yourselves. Do what it says." I
believe this sort of self-deception takes places in churches all over
the world. We have literally trained ourselves in self-deception. Let
me show you what I mean.

You go to the worship service on Sunday morning and hear a
powerful message on how we must love one another. You are literally brought to tears by the power and force of the message. And
you leave the service inspired and feeling so very good by what you
have heard.

The first steps of deception have taken place. It occurs when we
hear the Word preached, and feel good because we agree with it. For
so many of us, that's where it ends. No action taken. No doing of
the Word.

God's clear call to the Church is to be doers of His Word. James
goes on to give an illustration of what it is like to hear the Word and
then fail to act in obedience upon it.

"Anyone who listens to the word but does not do what it says is like a man who looks at his face in a mirror and, after looking at himself, goes away and immediately forgets what he looks like. But the man who looks intently into the perfect law that gives freedom, and continues to do this, not forgetting what he has heard, but doing it—he will be blessed in what he does" (James 1:23-25).

It is not hearing that changes us. It is acting on what we hear! We need to build the sort of expectancy in our lives and churches that what we hear we will begin to implement. When a sermon on loving one another is preached in a church, there should begin to be manifestations of that message all through the congregation. Christians will be inviting one another over for supper. Church members will be calling to see how they can pray for one another. Cards will be sent to other Christians encouraging and building them up. Christians will actually love one another, not just agreeing with a message they heard last Sunday.

James gives us a wonderful promise when we do the Word. He says in James 1:25 that the one who does the Word will be blessed in what he does. In other words, this will not be empty activity. When Christians make a commitment to walk in obedience to God's Word, God steps in to bless that commitment. As they do the Word, they receive blessing from God in that activity.

Paul describes what God will do in 1 Thessalonians 2:13: "And we also thank God continually because, when you received the word of God, which you heard from us, you accepted it not as the word of men, but as it actually is, the word of God, which is at work in you who believe." Listen to the implied promise of supernatural power here. The Word of God is actually at work in you. There is a partnership that begins to be effective when you act upon the Word of God. You begin to walk in obedience and the Word begins to work in you. The King James Version says the Word is "effective" in you.

That's what I want in my life—for God's Word to be effective in me. I want the promise of God that His Word would not return to

Him void . . . empty . . . ineffective. The power of God's Holy Spirit is set free in our lives as we move into the arena of being doers of the Word of God.

Prayer Focus: Ask the Lord to give you a love for His Word that results in obedience to His Word through the power of His Holy Spirit.

Prayer: Father, forgive me for the many times I have heard or read Your Word and failed to act upon it. Grant me a willing spirit to do, always through the strength of Your Spirit, what Your Word tells me to do.

Next Step: Take special notice of the next sermon you hear. Try to remember what the clear command of God for you is in the text of Scripture that is used. Determine to do what it says that next week.

DAY TWENTY-ONE

*"Your statutes are wonderful; therefore I will obey them. The
unfolding of your words gives light; it gives understanding to
the simple." (Psalm 119:129-130)*

Making a commitment to obeying God's Word will not only
change an individual but has the power to change a church
or an entire nation.

There is a wonderful example of that in the life of Josiah, King of
Judah. Young King Josiah had inherited a kingdom that had fallen
away from God. Idolatry and every kind of sin were rampant. Previous generations of kings had ignored the Word of God and followed
their own desires. Josiah, however, was different. The Scriptures say
that at age 16, Josiah began to seek the God of his ancestor David.
When he was 24, Josiah sent workers to the temple to begin cleaning and purifying it from the years of abuse and neglect. An astonishing discovery was made during the cleaning. The Book of the
Law given to Moses was found.

Josiah tore his robes in grief over this neglect of the Word of
God. Second Chronicles 34:21 records his words upon seeing the
long lost Scriptures: "Great is the LORD's anger that is poured out
on us because our fathers have not kept the word of the LORD; they
have not acted in accordance with all that is written in this book."

Josiah called together the leaders of Judah and all the inhabit-
ants of Jerusalem and read to them the words of the covenant. Look
at the king's response and that of his people to the reading of the
Word. "The king stood by his pillar and renewed the covenant in

the presence of the LORD—to follow the LORD and keep his commands, regulations and decrees with all his heart and all his soul, and to obey the words of the covenant written in this book. Then he had everyone in Jerusalem and Benjamin pledge themselves to it; the people of Jerusalem did this in accordance with the covenant of God, the God of their fathers" (34:31-32).

With this commitment to obey the Word, revival broke out in Judah. Idols were removed and Israel walked with God. There was a celebration of the Passover in Jerusalem like none ever seen as the people worshipped the Lord and rejoiced in the restoration of His Word.

God desires to once again revive His people. This revival will not come in just a burst of emotion, but in response to a praying people who have recommitted themselves to be doers of the Word of God.

Prayer Focus: Pray for the Word of God to be received with joy and trust by the members of your congregation.

Prayer: Father, the Bible tells us that You have exalted above all things, Your name and Your Word. Help me Lord to exalt Your name and Your Word by taking seriously all that You say. I commit myself to doing what You tell me to do through the power of Your Holy Spirit at work within me.

Next Step: You probably haven't lost your Bible like Israel did in the years before Josiah. But you might have "lost" a portion of scripture. This week, look at a book of the Bible that you may have been staying away from or just not noticing. Maybe one of the books written by an Old Testament prophet. Read that book this week and commit yourself to doing what that portion of God's Word tells you to do.

DAY TWENTY-TWO

"My soul thirsts for you, my body longs for you, in a dry and weary land where there is no water." (Psalm 63:1b)

Hunger and thirst are natural expressions of the basic human desire and need for food and water. One of the clear indicators that something is wrong physically is when we lose our appetite. It is the same spiritually. To hunger and thirst for God is at the very root of our being. It's the way God made us. When there is no hunger for the presence of God, it is an indicator that something is wrong spiritually. Because that hunger is so basic to human nature, it often finds fulfillment in other areas rather than in seeking God. Much as eating unhealthy junk food can dull physical appetite, so that which is not of God can dull our spiritual appetite.

This happens to non-Christians as they look for happiness and fulfillment in any area except in their relationship with God. It may be in human relationships, quest for power or money, or escape to physical pleasure. The saddest examples, however, are of Christians who allow their appetite for God to be dulled by other things, even religious things. Our churches are filled with believers who are so satiated by activities, programs and projects that they no longer have a hunger for God.

So many Christians today snack their way through the day on "junk-food" activities and then find they have no time to "feast" with God. We complain about our "busyness" and tiredness, but that is typically a spiritual problem more than a problem of schedule. We desire everything except God. We take God in small doses throughout the day and week and somehow hope that on Sunday we can "catch up" on our time with the Lord.

A key to revival in our own life will be the development of spiritual hunger and thirst for God. Conversely, a commitment must be made to lay aside lesser things in the quest for developing this godly desire for the presence of God Himself.

Prayer Focus: Ask the Lord to give you a hunger and thirst for Him that cannot be quenched by anything other than He Himself.

Prayer: Oh God, help me not to be satisfied by anything other than Your presence. Create a holy longing—a spiritual thirst for You that only You can satisfy.

Next Step: Give yourself a quick self-evaluation regarding desire. List the five things that give you greatest pleasure. Be honest. Start by asking the Lord to reveal truth in your inner man. Then, after you have made your list, present it to the Lord and ask Him to reorder your priorities according to His Heart.

DAY TWENTY-THREE

*"I spread out my hands to you; I thirst for you like a
parched land." (Psalm 143:6)*

God's Word is filled with passages that call us to desire for God.
I would suggest to you that one of, if not the most important
attribute of our life as a believer is simply to desire God. So often
our longing is for the things that God can give us rather than the
Lord Himself. If we are to experience revival in our own life as well
as in the Church, we must re-direct this desire.

Let's look at the Scriptures which speak of developing this hunger and thirst for God:

"Blessed are those who hunger and thirst for righteousness,
for they will be filled." (Matthew 5:6)
"Whoever drinks the water I give him will never thirst.
Indeed, the water I give him will become in him a spring of
water welling up to eternal life." (John 4:14)
"Then Jesus declared, 'I am the bread of life. He who comes
to me will never go hungry, and he who believes in me will
never be thirsty.'" (John 6:35)
"On the last and greatest day of the Feast, Jesus stood and
said in a loud voice, 'If anyone is thirsty, let him come to
me and drink. Whoever believes in me, as the Scripture has
said, streams of living water will flow from within him.'"
(John 7:37-38)
"Come, all you who are thirsty, come to the waters; and you

who have no money, come, buy and eat! Come, buy wine and milk without money and without cost. Why spend money on what is not bread, and your labor on what does not satisfy?" (Isaiah 55:1-2)

"O God, you are my God, earnestly I seek you; my soul thirsts for you, my body longs for you, in a dry and weary land where there is no water." (Psalm 63:1)

"The Spirit and the bride say, 'Come!' And let him who hears say, 'Come!' Whoever is thirsty, let him come; and whoever wishes, let him take the free gift of the water of life." (Revelation 22:17)

It is obvious that the imagery of hungering and thirsting after God is a much-used scriptural concept. From the prophets of the Old Testament to Jesus and on through to the book of Revelation, the people of God are depicted as those who have developed a desire for God. Could it be that the missing element in the Church today is that desire for God Himself?

Prayer Focus: Ask God to give you a holy desire for His presence this day that is beyond anything you have ever experienced.

Prayer: My Father and my Lord, how I long for You! More than life itself, I desire to walk daily in an intimate relationship with You. Thank You for placing that desire within me, and satisfying it by Your divine grace.

Next Step: Many of the Psalms are prayers of desire for God. They are often filled with phrases about seeking His face, or being thirsty for Him. Begin reading the Psalms, looking for those which speak of this desire. Select your favorites and begin praying them on a regular basis.

DAY TWENTY-FOUR

"My heart says of you, 'Seek His face!' Your face,
Lord, I will seek." (Psalm 27:8)

Ben Patterson writes, "Since the best teacher of prayer is the Holy Spirit, the best way to learn to pray is by praying. Whether, and how much we pray is, I think, finally a matter of appetite, of hunger for God and all that He is and desires."

C.S. Lewis wrote in *The Weight of Glory*, "We are far too easily pleased. That, in the end, is the reason we do not pray more than we do. Nothing less than infinite joy is offered us in God's kingdom of light. He has promised that we will one day shine like the sun in that kingdom (Matthew 13:43)."

In *Deepening Your Conversation with God*, Patterson says, "We have become satisfied with mere church, mere religious exertion, mere numbers and buildings—the things we can do. There is nothing wrong with these things, but they are no more than foam left by the surf on the ocean of God's glory and goodness."

How then, can we begin to develop that hunger for God? If we find ourselves lacking in desire, can it be rekindled within us? Perhaps the best way to look at this is to again make a comparison to physical hunger and the way we handle it. When we get hungry, many of us begin to look for something to appease the hunger. If we are at work, we may head to the snack machine in the hall, or if we are at home, we go to the cupboard or the refrigerator, looking for a snack that will take away the feeling of hunger. Hunger prompts us to seek something to fill us up, even if it is something that is not really good for us.

Spiritually speaking, there is a hunger for God that is often not recognized for what it is. It may be an empty feeling, a sense of longing, even loneliness in the midst of people. We start looking for ways to make the feeling go away, to fill up the emptiness. In a sense, we begin to look for the junk food that will mask the pangs of hunger within.

The danger of this type of behavior is that we dull our sense of hunger for God. In the same way that continued snacking through the day can dull our appetite and cause us to pass up a good, nutritious meal that our body needs, so we can fill up our schedules and desires to the point that we do not even realize that we no longer desire the presence of God.

It is no accident that one of the great spiritual disciplines of the Church is to fast. When we fast, we become acutely aware of our physical hunger. That physical hunger can lead to a spiritual hunger as well. Christians today are returning to fasting and prayer as a means of waking us up to our great need for the presence of God. It may be that we will need to fast from other things than food in order to restore our spiritual hunger. There may need to be a slowing of our hectic lifestyles that are crowding out our time with the Father. We may need to fast from some forms of entertainment to devote time to seeking the Lord. Those heavily involved in ministry may need to say "no" to that which is good, in order to seek that which is best. We may even need to reevaluate our family schedules.

Tommy Tenney, in his devotional, *Experiencing His Presence: Devotions for God Chasers*, prays a prayer that we all may need to use daily to build our hunger for God. "Lord Jesus, my soul aches at the mere mention of Your name. My heart leaps for every rumor of Your coming, and each possibility that You will manifest Your presence. I'm not satisfied with mere spiritual dainties. I'm ravenously hungry for You in Your fullness. I'm desperate to feast on the bread of Your presence and quench my thirst with the wine of Your Spirit."

May hungering and thirsting for God drive us to a passionate, relentless pursuit of Him.

Prayer Focus: Pray that the Lord would give you a never- ending desire to pursue His presence.

Prayer: Lord, I want to pray just like Tommy Tenney prayed in the prayer above. Make me ravenously hungry for You in Your fullness. Make me desperate to feast on the bread of Your presence and thirsty for the wine of Your Spirit.

Next Step: If you are physically able, set aside a day of fasting in order to develop a spiritual hunger for God. As your body desires food through the day, use those hunger pangs as prompts for prayer that cries out for the spiritual food and drink that truly satisfies.

DAY TWENTY-FIVE

"Now there were some Greeks among those who went up to worship at the Feast. They came to Philip, who was from Bethsaida in Galilee, with a request. 'Sir', they said, 'we would like to see Jesus.'" (John 12:20-21)

This is an amazing story in Scripture. At the same time that the religious leaders of the day were trying to silence Jesus, these Gentiles were trying to see Him. There is something about Jesus that draws people to Him, especially those who are free from traditional expectations. The Jews of that day were expecting a political Messiah who would free them from Roman rule. Jesus didn't match those expectations and consequently was rejected by His own people. But here are some Greeks—outsiders who have heard of this wonder-working rabbi from Galilee—and their desire is to see Him.

I think it is possible for those same factors to be at work today. The Lord's own people can become so used to church services and the way things have been that they fail to recognize Jesus. Sometimes it takes the "outsiders," those without a chutrch background to be the ones who develop a true passion to see the Lord. The story of the gospel is so new and amazing to them that they take seriously the commands to live out the life of Christ to a world that so desperately needs Him.

My question is: "Can we who have walked with Him for years, who have perhaps sat in church services for decades, still have that passion to see and know Him?" Obviously the answer is "Yes!" There are those who have continued to develop their love walk with the Lord even after many years. But there are many whose love has grown cold. So ultimately the questions are these: "How can we stoke the fires of passionate love for Jesus? How can we see the end better than the beginning? Can we who have known Him the longest, love Him the most?"

Scriptures teach us that rather than wearing out and growing cold in our love for the Lord, the exact opposite is to take place. Paul writes to the Corinthians, "And we, who with unveiled faces all reflect the Lord's glory, are being transformed into his likeness with ever-increasing glory, which comes from the Lord, who is the Spirit" (2 Corinthians 3:18). It is an ever-increasing glory that is to be occurring in our lives as we live out the live of faith.

What can keep this fire burning within us? I believe those Greeks who came to Philip had the key, whether they knew it or not. They said, "We would like to see Jesus."

Looking to Jesus is the answer. Longing to see Him is to be our basic desire. When Paul wrote to the Colossians he encouraged them to "set your hearts on things above, where Christ is seated at the right hand of God" (Colossians 3:1).

Prayer Focus: Ask the Lord to bring His transforming power to bear upon your innermost being.

Prayer: Lord, I would see You today. Give me the spiritual eyes to behold Your glory. Help me to keep my eyes fixed upon You.

Next Step: With pen in hand, read the Gospel of John in its entirety. Read slowly and prayerfully, asking this question: Lord, would You teach me more of Yourself as I read this inspired story of Your life? Write out the insights you receive as you read and pray.

DAY TWENTY-SIX

"Therefore, holy brothers and sisters, who share in the heavenly calling, fix your thoughts on Jesus, whom we acknowledge as our apostle and high priest." (Hebrews 3:1)

If we look to the Church, we may get discouraged. If we look to the task ahead, we may get weary. If we look to ourselves, we will give up. It is in looking to Jesus, in all His glory and sovereignty over all things, that everything falls into proper perspective.

Our difficulty is that even in the Lord's Church, we often look to everyone and everything but Jesus. We get so distracted by busyness and the affairs of this world that we forget to look to Jesus. As David Bryant said, we often find ourselves making Jesus our mascot instead of our monarch: He's around, but He's not in charge.

Oh, how the Church will be changed when we see Jesus for who He really is. Look what happened to the Apostle John when he saw Jesus in His glorified body: "Among the lamp stands was someone 'like a son of man,' dressed in a robe reaching down to his feet and with a golden sash around his chest. His head and hair were white like wool, as white as snow, and his eyes were like blazing fire. His feet were like bronze glowing in a furnace, and his voice was like the sound of rushing waters. In his right hand he held seven stars, and out of his mouth came a sharp double-edged sword. His face was like the sun shining in all its brilliance. When I saw him, I fell at his feet as though dead" (Revelation 1:13-17).

It is time for the Church of Jesus Christ to see Jesus! To see Him as He really is, not as a mascot, but as our monarch. Colossians

1:15-20 is perhaps the most powerful, vivid presentation in Scripture of who this Jesus, whom we worship, really is. "He is the image of the invisible God, the firstborn over all creation. For by him all things were created: things in heaven and on earth, visible and invisible, whether thrones or powers or rulers or authorities; all things were created by him and for him. He is before all things, and in him all things hold together. And he is the head of the body, the church; he is the beginning and the firstborn from among the dead, so that in everything he might have the supremacy. For God was pleased to have all his fullness dwell in him, and through him to reconcile to himself all things, whether things on earth or things in heaven, by making peace through his blood, shed on the cross."

When the Lord's own people turn their faces to heaven and begin to long to see Jesus, to develop that passion and hunger for His presence, then the Lord Himself will fulfill that longing with His own precious presence. Revival! Awakening! And those from the outside will begin to see and hear of this move of God in the midst of His people. Then, they will also begin to have the same request that Philip heard from those Greeks so long ago: "We would like to see Jesus."

"Nations will come to your light, and kings to the brightness of your dawn" (Isaiah 60:3).

Prayer Focus: Pray for the longing to see Jesus to be a passionate desire in your heart.

Prayer: In the midst of all the activities of my life, Lord would You give me a fresh perspective of who You are. Help me to settle for nothing less than You Yourself.

Next Step: Music has been used through the years to draw us near to the Lord. If you have a hymnal, take some time to browse through it and find favorites that speak of Jesus. Read or sing slowly and carefully through the words and use them to draw near to Him in prayer. If you don't have a hymnal, you can do the same thing on the internet by searching for hymns about Jesus.

DAY TWENTY-SEVEN

"Restore us, God Almighty; make your face shine on us, that we may be saved." (Psalm 80:7)

Revival comes to those who are desperate for it. Many today are talking about spiritual awakening and even beginning to pray about it. But have we allowed God to place within us the burden necessary to pray desperately for God to show up in our midst? Are we willing to "pray the price" to see God move in a powerful way in the Church today? As I continue to learn how to move my prayers into alignment with God's will, praying Scripture has become increasingly important. As I pray God's Word, I find myself praying in ways I would never have found myself praying before. So it is as we begin to place ourselves before the Lord in asking for a burden for revival. I have been greatly impacted by the prayer of Psalm 79.

This is a powerful prayer for revival. It was prayed from the broken heart of the psalmist, who saw the people of God under attack and the promises of God unfulfilled.

"O God, the nations have invaded your inheritance; they have defiled your holy temple, they have reduced Jerusalem to rubble. They have given the dead bodies of your servants as food to the birds of the air, the flesh of your saints to the beasts of the earth. They have poured out blood like water all around Jerusalem, and there is no one to bury the dead. We are objects of reproach to our neighbors, of scorn and derision to those around us. How long, O Lord? Will you be angry forever? How long will your jealousy burn like fire? Pour out your wrath on the nations that do not acknowledge you, on the kingdoms that do not call on your name; for they have devoured Jacob and destroyed his homeland. Do not hold against us the sins of the fathers; may your mercy come quickly to meet us, for we are in desperate need. Help us, O God our Savior, for the glory of your name; deliver us and forgive our sins for your name's sake. Why should the nations say, 'Where is their God?' Before our eyes, make known among the nations that you avenge the outpoured blood of your servants. May the groans of the prisoners come before you; by the strength of your arm preserve those condemned to die. Pay back into the laps of our neighbors seven times the reproach they have hurled at you, O Lord. Then we your people, the sheep of your pasture, will praise you forever; from generation to generation we will recount your praise."

Prayer Focus: Take Psalm 79 and pray it back to the Lord in your own words.

Prayer: Father, help me to pray with the passion and under-standing of this psalmist. Give me heaven's perspective on events that take place, both in the nations, and in those things right around my life. Give me the wisdom to pray for Your intervention.

Next Step: Make Psalm 79 your own prayer by paraphrasing it. Literally rewrite it and make it an expression of your own desires. Keep a copy of what you have written and pray it often.

DAY TWENTY-EIGHT

"Hear us, Shepherd of Israel, you who lead Joseph like a flock. You who sit enthroned between the cherubim, shine forth before Ephraim, Benjamin and Manasseh. Awaken your might; come and save us." (Psalm 80:1)

Praying through Psalm 79 is a great way to develop a biblical burden for revival. The text breaks down into a great outline for passionate prayer. Recognizing your current situation is a critical place to begin. The people of Israel were oppressed, under attack by their enemies. They finally got to a place of desperation—"for we are in desperate need" (v. 8). Until the Church today arrives at that place of desperation, we will never develop a burden for revival.

Get serious about the glory of God. Pagans were disparaging God because of the sorry situation of the Israelites. "Where is their God?" they asked. The fact that the world would ask such a question should bring great grief to God's people. In a very real sense, this is exactly what the world is saying of the Church today, "Where is your God?"

Recognition of your current situation and passion for God's glory will lead you to petition. It is at this point that you find Israel praying for mercy, deliverance, and forgiveness. It is a very personal sort of prayer that focuses on the needs of the people of God for restoration into the favor of God.

Taking the prayer a step further, we see the psalmist asking God to step into the situation. In a very real sense, the psalmist prays, "God, You answer the accusations of the enemy. By Your actions Lord, pay back the reproach that the world has heaped upon You through the sad condition of Your people."

The result of such a prayer is worship and praise. It's the natural result of seeing God work. Even before full-blown revival arrives, there is worship erupting from the people of God. And along with that is the commitment to pass it on to the next generation.

Praying such a prayer for revival is not a guarantee of revival. It is merely preparing the ground of the human heart for a fresh work of God. Praying with passion for revival begins to create a burden for revival among the Lord's people. And into such a prepared state, the Lord has often poured His rain from heaven.

Martyn Lloyd-Jones speaks of this preparatory work of prayer in his book, *Revival*: "Our essential trouble is that we are content with a very superficial and preliminary knowledge of God, His being, His cause. . . . We spend our lives in busy activism . . . instead of realizing our own failure, [that] we are not attracting anybody to Christ and that they probably see nothing in us that makes them desire to come to Him. The inevitable and constant preliminary to revival has always been in a thirst for God, a thirst, a living thirst for a knowledge of the living God and a longing and a burning desire to see Him acting, manifesting Himself and His power, rising and scattering His enemies . . . the thirst for God and the longing for the exhibition of His glory are the essential preliminaries to revival" (pp. 90-91).

May our prayers for revival develop a great thirst for God, not only in our own lives, but in the lives of those around us.

Prayer Focus: Bring before the Lord prayers of repentance that we so often find ourselves busy serving Him, but not busy seeking Him.

Prayer: Lord, may Your Holy Word format my prayers for revival. Give me a great concern for Your glory and Your reputation. Even as I pray for revival, may I first be consumed by zeal for You and Your house.

Next Step: Scripture memorization is often a thing of our childhood rather than a part of today. Bringing God's Word into your heart can greatly enrich your prayer life. Memorize Psalm 79:9, "Help us, God our Savior, for the glory of your name; deliver us and forgive our sins for your name's sake."

DAY TWENTY-NINE

"All that we have accomplished, you have done for us."
(Isaiah 26:12)

It is so easy for most of us to get caught up in seeing our Christian faith as unending activity. Attending meetings, serving, meeting needs, developing ministry skills, all can become the center of who we are as Christians. When that happens, our focus has shifted off of Christ—who He is and what He has done for us—and begins to be on who we are and what we are doing for Him. That is never a spiritually healthy situation.

God is always trying to teach us to depend upon Him. It is never about us. It's always about Him. Jesus told us that apart from Him, we could do nothing (John15:5). Most of us have to be convinced of that by bitter experience.

We try so hard to do ministry. We plan and strategize and budget and dream of all we will do in the kingdom of God. In a very real sense, those things are admirable. One of our great joys is in serving the Lord. Where we go wrong is when we try to do this in our own strength.

One of the very real reasons for prayerlessness in the Church is our failure to realize our dependence upon Jesus. We want to try it our way first, and then pray when our way gets is in trouble. One of the most practical aspects of prayer is the way it teaches us to lean upon the Lord. Ronnie Floyd, in *How to Pray*, says there are two critical aspects to remember about prayer: 1) Prayer occurs when you depend on God, and 2) Prayerlessness occurs when you depend on yourself.

A praying church is a church that has learned to depend upon God. A praying Christian is one who has learned to depend upon God. The crying need of our day is not more religious activity, but for Christians who will trust the Lord and serve Him out of a greater dependency upon Him.

Prayer Focus: Repent of the sin of prayerlessness. Receive the Lord's forgiveness and commit yourself to depend upon Him in prayer.

Prayer: Father, forgive me for trying to do Your work in my own strength. Teach me to pray on all occasion with all kind of prayers. Help me to walk in complete dependence upon You.

Next Step: Have you ever looked at prayerlessness as sin? If you've repented of this sin, how will your prayer life look in future days? Remember, it isn't so much a matter of how much time, as simply learning to walk and talk with Jesus throughout the day.

DAY THIRTY

"The Lord replied, 'My Presence will go with you, and I will give you rest.'" (Exodus 33:14)

Those of us committed to revival often want to jump into activity to bring about revival. In the midst of our busyness and religious activity, Isaiah speaks words that both condemn and comfort.

"This is what the Sovereign LORD, the Holy One of Israel, says: 'In repentance and rest is your salvation, in quietness and trust is your strength'" (Isaiah 30:15).

Repentance is the first response for those who have accepted the truth of who Jesus is. When the crowd heard Peter speak of Christ on the Day of Pentecost, they literally interrupted his sermon with the question, "Brothers, what shall we do?" Peter's first word in response is, "Repent." There is more, but repentance is first.

What Christians often fail to understand is that repentance is not just a one-time event. It becomes a way of life. As we sin, we are continually called to repent, to turn from our rebellion and move back into a way of life that pleases God. Repentance is in such a primary place because it makes us aware that we cannot in any way earn our salvation. We are dependent upon the mercy of God.

As a matter of fact, our repentance will often be about the fact that we have forgotten how dependent we are upon the Lord. I know that for me, it seems that I must again and again come to God, repenting of my tendency to try to do ministry in my own strength. It is crucial then, that we understand why Isaiah put together repentance and rest. The rest spoken of here is not inactivity. Rather it is an awareness that the only thing that counts is God's work, often through us. Not our work, but His strength and power accomplishing what He desires through His servants.

The author of Hebrews spends the entire fourth chapter dealing with the Sabbath rest of the people of God. In verse 10 he writes, "for anyone who enters God's rest also rests from his own work." As we rest from our works, God's work is highlighted and He receives all the glory and praise. We enter into His rest, which is not a cessation of activity on our part, but an awareness that God is at work and that we are called to allow His work to progress within us. To make it simple, it is us going back to the words of Jesus in John 15:5, "Apart from me, you can do nothing."

So we repent, because we have not entered God's rest. We have tried to build our own kingdoms, in our own strength, and somehow procure our own salvation. We repent, and rest, and when we move away from God's rest (and we will), we repent again and move back into God's rest. This Isaiah says, is your salvation, depending upon the saving power of Christ and His continued work within you.

The second half of Isaiah's instruction is another way of saying the same thing. In quietness and trust is your strength. We don't often think of our words as tools or weapons, but we certainly do try to change circumstances and people by our use of words. How many times have you tried to talk someone into or out of something. We sense that there is a power in our words to change people's lives. It is so! Words can heal or harm, comfort or correct, delight or destroy. We are warned over and over again in Scripture about the power of words.

So often, we find ourselves using words to defend, attack, or manipulate a situation, instead of trusting in the Lord. Developing a spirit of quietness is an essential part of learning to trust in the Lord. If we are always speaking into a situation, we often will be excluding the Lord from accomplishing what He desires.

Being quiet is difficult. But silence is a palpable way of expressing faith. When Jesus was hauled before the authorities, He fulfilled Old Testament Scriptures which prophesied of Him, "He was oppressed and afflicted, yet he did not open his mouth; he was led like a lamb to the slaughter, and as a sheep before her shearers is silent, so he did not open his mouth" (Isaiah 53:7). He trusted the situation to His heavenly Father.

Quietness implies not only control of our tongue, but control of our life. It is stepping off the merry-go-round of constant activity in life and allowing the Lord to lead us beside still waters. Quietness is a concrete example of trusting the Lord, and in so doing, depending upon His strength to do and be all that God desires.

There is a great call from heaven to the Church today. It is a call for increased intimacy with the Lord. It is a call back into the presence of God. The way to respond to this call from God is through repentance, rest, quietness and trust.

Prayer Focus: Spend time today preparing your heart for all that God has for you as you continue to live your life for His glory.

Prayer: Lord, help me today to be still and know that You are God. May I delight in You and Your work. Help me to trust completely in You in all things.

Next Step: This may take a bit of planning, but it will be worth it. Schedule a day of solitude and quiet. For many with families this will require help from others. For many others, such a day means giving up a precious day off from work. Take a day and give it completely to the Lord. Keep silent and as much as possible, refrain from interaction with others. It will be a day you will never forget!

REVIVAL PRAYING AS A WAY OF LIFE

For many years now, a committed core of Christians have been praying for revival in the United States. Believing that it is the will of God for our nation to experience heaven-sent spiritual awakening, they have poured out their hearts before Him in sincere intercession. Still, we find ourselves in the midst of spiritual dryness and church-as-usual. Some Christian leaders have pointed out that a large part of the problem lies in our lack of repentance. Revival will not come without tears of repentance.

All too many Christians view potential revival as a nice thing to have as long as it doesn't interfere with anything we've already scheduled. There's been an appalling lack of passion or desire for awakening. Some would say we have not been desperate enough to have revival.

I believe that is beginning to change. As I travel to churches all across the nation, I am seeing an increased awareness of the desperate situation in the Church and in the nation. The rapid moral slide of our culture has grabbed the attention of many believers. Revival is quickly being seen as our only hope.

Much of the problem however, lies in our national tendency for quick fixes. Let's have revival and get everything back to normal so we can go on with our own lifestyle. God will not send revival to those with such an attitude. The desperation isn't so much for a changed culture as it is a desperation for God Himself.

A Fresh Experience of Christ

Christians who long for revival are ultimately longing for a fresh experience of Christ. That's why they will see that it is not a quick fix of praying for a while until something happens. It is instead, a way of life in which we continually cry out to God and seek His Face.

My challenge to you as you complete these thirty days of prayer for revival is to make this your way of praying for the rest of your life. Thirty days is good, but it's just a start. My prayer is that these days will help you to develop a habit or pattern of revival praying that will continue for years to come. The passionate seeking after the Lord is in itself an aspect of personal revival and spiritual awakening.

If we are to persevere in praying for revival, we must have a clear vision regarding what we are praying toward. I love the description given by Raymond Ortlund, Jr of what revival could look like: "When God rends the heavens and comes down on His people, a divine power achieves what human effort at its best, fails to do. God's people thirst for the ministry of the Word and receive it with tender meetings of soul. The grip of enslaving sin is broken. Reconciliation between believers is sought and granted. Spiritual things, rather than material things, capture people's hearts. A defensive, timid church is transformed into a confident army. Believers joyfully suffer for their Lord. They treasure usefulness to God over career advancement. Communion with God is avidly enjoyed. Church and Christian organizations reform their policies and procedures. People who had always been indifferent to the gospel now inquire anxiously. And this type of spiritual movement draws in not just the isolated straggler here and there but large numbers of people. A wave of divine grace washes over the church and spills onto the world. That is what happens when God comes."

Do you believe that God wants all of this for His Church? Do you believe that the Lord is wanting a purified Bride, made holy and prepared for His Coming? The psalmist cries out in Psalm 85:6, "Will you not revive us again?" Is that your heart cry as well?

Christians around the nation are beginning to understand our desperate straits and are crying out to God for revival. Will you join us in daily, fervent prayer for spiritual awakening in the United States and around the world? You can impact your own local congregation by adding these prayer points to your prayers:

- Pray for a spirit of prayer in your congregation.
- Pray that repentance becomes a way of life for your congregation.
- Pray that your church will experience the presence of Christ in a fresh, new way.

"O Lord, will you not rend the heavens and come down? Come down to make your name known to your people." We, Your people, are desperate for a fresh sense of Your presence and Your power to save and purify.

Have mercy on us, O God!

About twenty years ago, my friend Bob Bakke discovered something he refers to as The National Prayer Accord as he was working on his doctorate on the history of the Great Awakening here in this nation. It is a rhythm of prayer where people pray weekly, monthly, quarterly, annually for revival. The National Prayer Committee, and a number of other prayer leaders and organizations, believe that we need to begin rebuilding this rhythm of prayer into our lives.

What this means is that on a weekly basis each of us prays for revival, either by ourselves or with a small group of believers. We do this not just for six months or a year, but until we see God move. This is not a short-term solution or the latest fad, but something we build into our prayer lives. On a monthly basis our congregation comes together and we cry out for revival. On a quarterly basis, we gather the churches that will in our area to come together to pray for revival. And then annually on the National Day of Prayer we come together to cry out to God for revival.

I believe God is calling every one of us here to build this rhythm into our prayers and into our lives. But let me suggest to you that is just the framework. My vision is that we are going to see day and night extraordinary prayer in fulfillment of Isaiah 62 that will usher in the next move of God. As the Lord says,

"I have posted watchmen on your walls, O Jerusalem; they will never be silent day or night. You who call on the LORD, give yourselves no rest, and give Him no rest till He establishes Jerusalem and makes her the praise of the earth" (Isaiah 62:6-7).

God is not calling just for weekly prayer meetings, but for extraordinary prayer, such as in the book of Acts where they gathered for ten days and at the end of that God poured out His Spirit in mighty power. And they did not quit praying, but they gathered regularly, even daily, and prayed. They spent time with their resurrected Lord in prayer and during one of those times the very building shook with the power of God that was present. May we have shaking buildings again! May we see the power of God poured out in our day!

Note: You can see the entire National Prayer Accord at: national-prayeraccord.com